GEORGE BELLOWS
PAINTER WITH A PUNCH!

Robert Burleigh

Published in association with the National Gallery of Art, Washington

ABRAMS BOOKS FOR YOUNG READERS · NEW YORK

Start punching, Tiger!"

"Hook 'im, Red!"

The densely packed room crackles with catcalls and gruff yells. Smoke rises toward the low ceiling. On the raised platform at the room's center, two men bob and weave, jabbing and pummeling each other with muscular arms. The white-shirted referee separates the fighters and then quickly leaps out of the way. "Go!"

The battle rages on.

Pow! Boom! Blood runs down one man's twisted face.

It's Fight Night at Sharkey's.

The crowd leans toward the ring. Individual shouts join together in a jagged roar. The spectators' eyes are as intense as those of the two boxers.

Stag at Sharkey's The fighters battle head-to-head and toe-to-toe! Painted in 1909, this realistic picture of a boxing bout at Sharkey's Saloon became George Bellows's best-known painting. It captures the gritty underworld of New York City that George and other artists tried to capture in the early years of the twentieth century.

PREVIOUS PAGE George Bellows, approximately eleven years old.

One man—seated at ringside—observes the events somewhat differently. He watches closely both the fury of the fighters and the fans' reactions. But who wins the bout doesn't matter to him. He has his own goal: to wrestle a picture from the chaotic scene, to capture the wild energy of this moment!

Is this strange? An artist here, in a smelly, grungy saloon?

Shouldn't an artist search for *beautiful* things to paint? Golden sunsets? Quiet, tree-lined rivers? Or perhaps a wealthy gentleman, or a celebrity dressed in her finest clothes? Many people would say just that.

But not George Bellows. It's New York in the early 1900s, and to George, the many moods of his adopted city—beautiful and ugly— are all pictures calling out to be painted. Subjects for great paintings, he believes, are everywhere, and he is determined to find them!

The fight is over. The crowd disperses. George walks home alone through the dark, silent streets. The remarkable scene he has just witnessed replays in his mind. In his room, an empty canvas, propped on an easel, is waiting. "The way to become a painter," he reminds himself once again, "is to paint." There is so much work to do!

Approach to the Bridge at Night This painting uses powerful contrasts of dark and light to show how mysterious the city looks at night. The Manhattan Bridge is seen by moonlight in the distance while streetlights illuminate a row of buildings in the middle ground and a horse-drawn carriage at the bottom left.

To become an athlete . . . or an artist? For George Bellows, born in 1882 and growing up in Columbus, Ohio, it is not an easy choice. Why? Because young George is both.

Tall for his age, George takes easily to the game of basketball. But baseball is his first love. An infielder who bats left-handed, he delights in the crack of the bat against the pitched ball. Pure music! he thinks. (Some people in Columbus believe he will make it to the major leagues.)

But George shows even rarer skill as an artist. When not playing basketball or baseball, he often sits on his front steps and sketches, sometimes while others watch. His amazed friends say that George can draw just about anything!

George as a member of the Central High School baseball team. During the 1900 season, Bellows (*front row, left*) played second base.

Then, at the age of twenty-two, George Bellows makes a decision. Suddenly—and against the wishes of his father, a business-man—he drops out of college before grad-uating, packs a suitcase, and leaves for the largest, most energetic city in America: New York. His goal: to become a great artist.

Turn-of-the-century New York City teems with life. George Bellows walks excitedly down the long avenues lined with mansions of the rich, where stylish horse-drawn buggies still compete with newfangled motor cars. There are subway trains! There are electric trolleys! There are early skyscrapers, too, looming like the prows of giant ships!

New York George Bellows's painting *New York* is, like the city itself, so crowded with people, animals, buildings, signs, streets, and more that it is hard to believe the picture is only five feet wide. The time is around 1910, and horse-drawn carts compete with electric streetcars and throngs of pedestrians. (Part of the congestion is no doubt caused by the fact that the traffic light has not yet been invented!)

9

George enrolls at the New York School of Art. Located just around the corner is a YMCA, where he finds cheap accommodations. Art school is pure joy. Here he meets a teacher he will never forget. Robert Henri is an artist, but he is also an inspiring instructor who is able to instill in his students the belief that art matters more than anything else.

Classes are prank-filled and fun. Students often compete to see who can do the most one-finger chin-ups while hanging from the top edge of an open door! But the classes are also deeply serious. "What does an artist do?" Henri asks. "An artist disturbs, upsets, enlightens," he says, answering his own question. "And anything that strikes you as real is worthy of being painted."

George listens, looks, and learns. He sees that painting can be a great adventure. He becomes what Henri calls a "sketch hunter." When not in class, George wanders the streets, looking for new or different scenes to paint. Excited, alert, he feels his life is beginning in a completely new way.

No other artist meant more to George than his early instructor, the painter and teacher Robert Henri (OPPOSITE). Henri encouraged his students to look for new subjects everywhere, especially on the streets of New York. Henri's own 1902 painting, *Snow in New York* (ABOVE), pictures a bleak winter scene.

Cliff Dwellers Around the turn of the twentieth century, thousands of European immigrants arrived in New York every day. They often lived in tenement buildings that were compared to mountain cliffs. In *Cliff Dwellers*, George Bellows brings to life the hurly-burly world of one densely packed "canyon."

George's long walks take him everywhere. He passes the homes of the wealthy, whose facades are marked by tall marble pillars. He crosses bridges, stopping to gaze far downriver to where large and small vessels come and go. He stops at crowded restaurants. He pauses in parks.

Most of all, he strolls through the densely packed slums of New York's Lower East Side. Here, immigrants from many parts of the world struggle to make their way. And here, the streets are never still. Men with lunch buckets trudge off to dark shops, where they work long hours for little pay. Women retrieve breeze-blown wash from lines that extend from one tenement (an apartment building) to the next. Rusty fire escapes zigzag down the buildings' peeling sides.

There are shouts, there are smells, there is music from an organ grinder, there are open windows with fluttering curtains, and there are old people sitting on the steps. And there are children—always children—seeking freedom from narrow, stifling, crowded rooms. They swarm about, laughing, calling, stealing rides on passing wagons, inventing games (fighting, too!), and jostling for places on the cracked sidewalks.

George's mind races. Images burn into his brain. The energy! The heartbeat! The hope! The city seems to be calling out: *Look. See. Paint me. Paint me as I really am.*

Wandering one day along the edge of the East River, George spots a group of boys swimming. Aha! When he returns to his studio, he paints the scene. The painting, titled *River Rats,* shows the swimmers frolicking in the water at the bottom of a steep bluff, with the street and tall buildings looming above.

River Rats shows the unmistakable signs of many of George Bellows's paintings: A sense of action. An unusual point of view. Rapid brushstrokes. And a feeling for the lives of ordinary people.

A second painting of swimmers, *Forty-Two Kids*, pictures boys preparing to dive into the water off a broken-down wooden dock. This painting is selected by the Pennsylvania Academy of the Fine Arts for a $300 prize. But almost immediately the prize is taken back and given to another painter. Why? Many people conclude it was because George's painting showed most of the subjects without clothes—a no-no in the genteel art world of the time!

Splinter Beach On a public dock in Brooklyn, groups of kids play, roughhouse, and dive headfirst into the East River in the shadow of the Brooklyn Bridge. This drawing by George Bellows is similar to his paintings *River Rats* and *Forty-Two Kids*. In each he shows the children of a teeming city escaping from the confines of their surroundings, if only briefly.

Frankie, the Organ Boy
Bellows loved the inhabitants of the crowded New York streets. Wandering and ever alert, he often came across interesting people whom he wanted to paint, like Frankie, an organist and street performer.

John Sloan, *Six O'Clock, Winter* (OPPOSITE) Bellows was not the only artist interested in capturing the darker side of contemporary New York. John Sloan was one of the so-called Ashcan School of painters. In this painting, a faceless crowd moves through the gathering dusk as an elevated train roars overhead.

George keeps exploring street life. He loves the bright-eyed, confident, cocky children he passes along the way. He paints, draws, etches their portraits: *Laughing Boy*; *Frankie, the Organ Boy*; *Paddy Flannigan.* The rough flow of the paint on the canvas seems to match the subjects' rough-and-ready lives.

George's paintings gain attention. He is among a group of artists who focus on the less romantic parts of the city, like bars, train stations, movie theaters, and alleyways. Two other such artists are John Sloan (1871–1951) and Everett Shinn (1876–1953). Reviewers attack the group, calling them "apostles of ugliness" because they dare to paint the seamier side of life. (Some years later, and for the same reason, a number of these artists will be grouped together under the heading "the Ashcan School.")

But a few reviewers find complimentary things to say about George's art. They especially praise his ability to convey strong feelings in his work. "It's in bad taste," one says, "but it's life—and that is the main thing."

George continues to roam the city far and wide. The rivers of New York capture his interest, and many paintings result. One of them, *North River*, pictures the Hudson River. In the painting, a ferryboat steams over the blue water toward the near shore, where tiny figures, hardly more than daubs of black paint, await its arrival. By putting in such small, contrasting figures, George is able to suggest the immense size of the whole scene.

George is thrilled when the Pennsylvania Academy of the Fine Arts decides to buy this painting! It is his first sale, and it earns him $250.

By 1906, George is living in a larger space, helped somewhat by a small allowance from his once-reluctant father. It is located on the sixth (and top) floor of a building and is called Studio 616. He works with great speed, often finishing a painting in a single day. Concentrating intensely on the canvas, he darts back and forth (not unlike a boxer on the attack!), stopping only to sit in his favorite rocking chair and reflect on his progress.

North River (ABOVE) Bellows's canvases often manage to give a sense of vastness and immensity. In *North River*, the viewer sees everything from the far-off horizon to still-distant people to the very nearby landscape, as a boat churns its way through icy waters. The sense of isolation and rugged nature contrasts with the fact that the scene is actually close to urban New York City.

Bellows in his studio, 1908 (LEFT) George Bellows relaxes in the upper-floor studio where he painted many of his famous New York scenes. (He slept in an adjoining room.) The rocker in the foreground was a kind of "meditation chair" that he liked to sit in when taking a break to study his work.

Because George is easygoing and loves to laugh, many friends stop by. They include the painter Rockwell Kent, the young actor Clifton Webb (later a famous movie star), and the man who will become America's most renowned playwright, Eugene O'Neill.

An even more important friend visits, too. Emma Story is a young New Jersey woman who is interested in the arts. She and George fall in love and, after a long courtship, marry in 1910. Though not an artist herself, Emma joins George on many of his wanderings through the city. In the summers they travel together to nearby Long Island or up to Maine. They relax in the countryside while George paints the local scene.

Emma at the Piano George had a rich baritone voice and loved to sing, especially when accompanied on the piano by his wife, Emma. He painted many portraits of her (and of their two daughters), and this one, with Emma's dark blue dress seeming to melt into the black background, is one of the best.

Often in need of money, George joins a semi-pro baseball team that schedules games around the city. Catchers are paid more because of the danger of standing unprotected behind the batter, so George converts himself from an infielder to a catcher! But no matter how many games he plays or how many practices he must attend, he always finds time to sketch and paint.

Like all New Yorkers, George is fascinated by the many construction sites, which are busy day and night. It's an age of vast building projects in the city. To construct Pennsylvania Station, entire blocks are cleared, and two long train tunnels are built under the Hudson River to New Jersey. George's painting *Blue Morning* shows the frenzied activity of workers digging the huge hole that will become the train station itself.

Blue Morning A crane arm lifts, men bend and hammer, and dust clouds rise. New York's Pennsylvania Station is being built! George Bellows's paintings often have the feeling of a photograph.

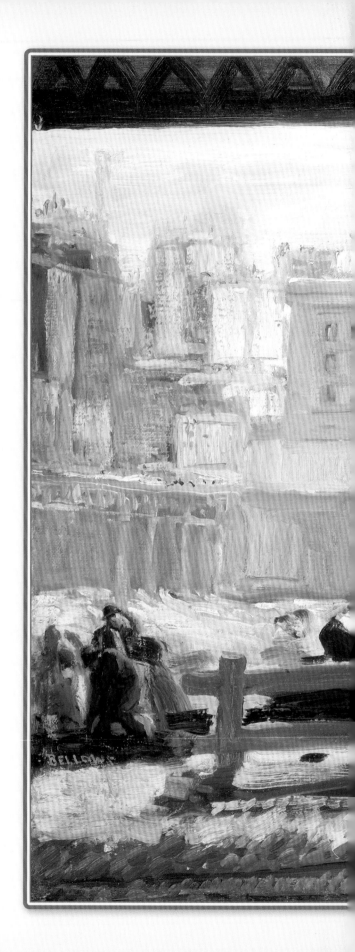

On another walk, George notices a desolate building standing on its own under a bridge that crosses the East River. Back in the studio, he paints this view, calling it *The Lone Tenement.* "It's me at my best," he thinks.

During the early twentieth century, boxing is illegal in New York. Many city leaders feel the sport is too violent to be encouraged by public showings. But this doesn't stop George Bellows. With many others, he attends bouts held in the back rooms of saloons (renamed "clubs" for the occasion). While the crowd roars and waves scorecards, George looks on and commits the scene to memory.

The Lone Tenement This single tenement is the last building in a neighborhood that once held four hundred such structures. Bellows's painting emphasizes the looming presence of the building, as well as the underside of the huge bridge that passes over it.

"I don't know anything about boxing," he likes to say. Yet the paintings he makes based on these fights will become his best-known works. Some critics note that the figures in the paintings are awkwardly drawn or that the ringside spectators have odd, caricatured faces. What concerns George most, though, is creating a "you-are-there" feeling. And this he surely does. Paintings such as *Both Members of This Club* and *Stag at Sharkey's* have, as one art reviewer says, a raw power that "hits you between the eyes."

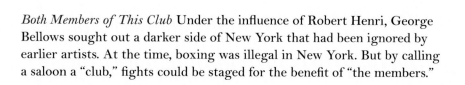

Both Members of This Club Under the influence of Robert Henri, George Bellows sought out a darker side of New York that had been ignored by earlier artists. At the time, boxing was illegal in New York. But by calling a saloon a "club," fights could be staged for the benefit of "the members."

George's reputation among artists and critics continues to grow. One morning in 1909, a letter arrives. George opens it. It tells him that he has just been elected an associate member of the National Academy of Design, an honorary association of American artists, located in New York. George is one of the youngest persons ever to be so honored! Prizes and awards follow. He is asked to submit paintings to important exhibitions. His work begins to sell more often. He is also appointed an instructor at the Art Students League, one of the city's most prestigious art schools.

George's freedom with his paintbrush extends to his political views as well. Starting in 1911, his liberal stance on various social issues leads him to serve on the editorial board of the socialist magazine *The Masses* and also to contribute illustrations to it. He breaks ranks with many of his fellow socialists, however, when he later supports America's entrance into World War I.

In ten years, George Bellows goes from being an unknown painter to being one of the most highly regarded young artists in America, acclaimed for his "truthfulness of observation" and "startling reality." The city he has adopted has at last truly adopted him.

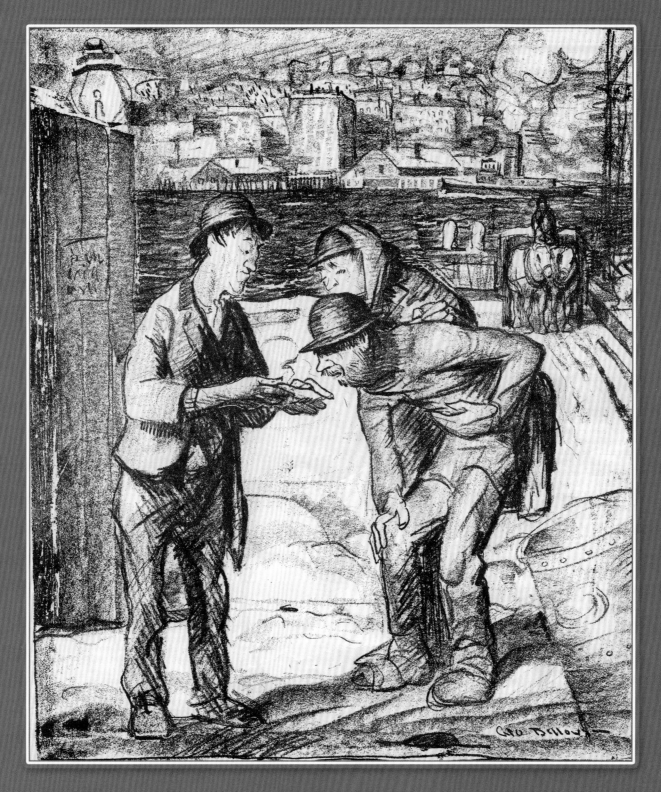

Real Tragedy Bellows not only painted for the general public, he also drew illustrations for the magazine *The Masses*. The magazine stood up for the rights of working people at a time when few publications did. Here, three hungry, jobless men have been forced to scavenge for food in a garbage can.

In 1917, when the United States enters World War I, George considers his future. Although he wants to join the tank corps, he is older now, and the father of two daughters, and he does not serve in the armed forces.

The next few years are filled with many paintings—landscapes, portraits, and a series of prints and paintings depicting the horrors of the war.

Then suddenly in early 1925, George begins to feel knife-like pains in his side. Accustomed to sports injuries that simply fade away, he refuses to go to a hospital—until it is too late. Appendicitis strikes. Within days, George Bellows is dead at the age of forty-two.

Lady Jean George Bellows didn't paint only the rougher side of urban life. He and his wife had two daughters, Anne and Jean. Here, George, in one of his last paintings, has captured their younger daughter, Jean, dressed up.

Self-Portrait George Bellows carefully registers the intense gaze of an artist trying to capture every detail of his subject. George took the same care with all his pictures, whether street scenes done from memory or portraits done in the studio.

What George might have accomplished had he lived longer is, of course, unknown. The *New York Times*, in a praise-filled obituary, stated that he "died before his work was done." Still, George Bellows's output was considerable. He dared to explore bold, new subjects, and he left an artistic record of New York City during a fascinating time in its history a hundred years ago. And, finally, he created paintings that are a permanent contribution to the history of American art. George, in his easygoing way, might call that "a knockout!"

ACKNOWLEDGMENTS

With special thanks to Charles Brock, Associate Curator of American and British Paintings; Karen Sagstetter, Senior Editor; Magda Nakassis, Assistant Editor; and Judy Metro, Editor in Chief—all at the National Gallery of Art—as well as Howard Reeves, Editor-at-Large; Jenna Pocius, Editorial Assistant; Maria Middleton, Senior Designer; and Jim Armstrong, Managing Editor—all of Abrams Books.

WHERE TO SEE WORKS BY GEORGE BELLOWS

UNITED STATES

Arkansas
Crystal Bridges Museum of American Art, Bentonville

California
Fine Arts Museums of San Francisco
Los Angeles County Museum of Art
San Diego Museum of Art
Santa Barbara Museum of Art

Connecticut
Yale University Art Gallery, New Haven

Florida
Harn Museum of Art, University of Florida, Gainesville
Norton Museum of Art, West Palm Beach

Georgia
High Museum of Art, Atlanta
Telfair Museums, Savannah

Illinois
The Art Institute of Chicago
Cedarhurst Center for the Arts, Mt. Vernon
Block Museum of Art, Northwestern University, Evanston

Indiana
Ball State University Museum of Art, Muncie
Brauer Museum of Art, Valparaiso University, Valparaiso
Indianapolis Museum of Art
Swope Art Museum, Terre Haute

Kansas
Nelson-Atkins Museum of Art, Kansas City
Wichita Art Museum

Maine
Colby College Museum of Art, Waterville
Farnsworth Art Museum, Rockland
Monhegan Museum, Monhegan Island
Portland Museum of Art

Massachusetts
Addison Gallery of American Art, Andover
Harvard Art Museums, Cambridge
Museum of Fine Arts, Boston
Williams College Museum of Art, Williamstown
Worcester Art Museum

Michigan
Detroit Institute of Arts

Minnesota
Minneapolis Institute of Arts

Mississippi
Lauren Rogers Museum of
Art, Laurel

New Jersey
Montclair Art Museum

New York
Brooklyn Museum
Memorial Art Gallery,
University of Rochester
The Metropolitan Museum
of Art, New York City
The Museum of Modern Art,
New York City
National Academy Museum &
School, New York City
Whitney Museum of
American Art,
New York City

North Carolina
North Carolina Museum of
Art, Raleigh

Ohio
Butler Institute of American
Art, Youngstown
Canton Museum of Art

Cleveland Museum of Art
Columbus Museum of Art
Springfield Museum of Art
Toledo Museum of Art

Oklahoma
Oklahoma City Museum of
Art

Pennsylvania
Carnegie Museum of Art,
Pittsburgh
Pennsylvania Academy of the
Fine Arts, Philadelphia

Rhode Island
Museum of Art, Rhode
Island School of Design,
Providence

Tennessee
Hunter Museum of American
Art, Chattanooga

Texas
Amon Carter Museum of
American Art, Fort Worth
Blanton Museum of Art,
University of Texas
at Austin
Dallas Museum of Art
Museum of Fine Arts,
Houston

Virginia
Chrysler Museum of Art,
Norfolk
Maier Museum of Art
at Randolph College,
Lynchburg
Virginia Museum of Fine
Arts, Richmond

Washington
Frye Art Museum, Seattle

Washington, D.C.
Corcoran Gallery of Art
Hirshhorn Museum and
Sculpture Garden
National Gallery of Art
Phillips Collection
Smithsonian American Art
Museum

Wisconsin
Chazen Museum of Art,
University of Wisconsin–
Madison
Milwaukee Art Museum

CANADA
Ontario
Art Gallery of Ontario,
Toronto

SPAIN
Thyssen-Bornemisza
Museum, Madrid

35

SOURCE NOTES

page 4 "The way . . . to paint": George Bellows, quoted in Mary Sayre Haverstock, *George Bellows: An Artist in Action* (New York: Merrell, 2007), p. 29.

page 10 "What does an artist . . . being painted." Robert Henri, quoted in Charles H. Morgan, *George Bellows, Painter of America* (New York: Reynal), 1965, p. 40.

page 18 "It's in bad taste . . . main thing." Quoted in Haverstock, *George Bellows*, p. 40.

page 25 "It's me . . . best." George Bellows, quoted in Haverstock, *George Bellows*, p. 56.

page 26 "hits you . . . the eyes." Quoted in Morgan, *George Bellows*, p. 104.

page 28 "truthfulness of observation," "startling reality." Quoted in Morgan, *George Bellows*, p. 83.

BIBLIOGRAPHY

Braider, Donald. *George Bellows and the Ashcan School of Painting*. Garden City, N.Y.: Doubleday, 1971.

Doezema, Marianne. *George Bellows and Urban America*. New Haven: Yale University Press, 1992.

Haverstock, Mary Sayre. *George Bellows: An Artist in Action*. New York: Merrell Publishers, 2007.

Morgan, Charles H. *George Bellows, Painter of America*. New York: Reynal, 1965.

Quick, Michael, et al. *The Paintings of George Bellows*. New York: Abrams, 1992.

Young, Mahonri Sharp. *The Paintings of George Bellows*. New York: Watson-Guptill, 1973.

COVER ILLUSTRATION (OPPOSITE): *Dempsey and Firpo* is one of George Bellows's most famous boxing paintings. It shows Jack Dempsey, the world heavyweight champion, being knocked out of the ring in the first round by challenger Luis Ángel Firpo of Argentina. (Dempsey climbed back into the ring with assistance and was later proclaimed the winner of the fight, although controversy remains over who really won.) Bellows's painting was completed in 1924, about a year after the fight and just a few months before the artist died. To highlight the drama, the painting places the viewer in the first row, looking up at the intense action.

ILLUSTRATION CREDITS

Cover (detail) and left (in full): George Bellows, *Dempsey and Firpo*, 1924, oil on canvas, Whitney Museum of American Art, New York, purchase with funds from Gertrude Vanderbilt Whitney, 31.95.

Title page: George Bellows, c. 1893, George Bellows Papers, Amherst College Archives and Special Collections, Amherst, Massachusetts; by permission of the Trustees of Amherst College.

pages 2–3: George Bellows, *Stag at Sharkey's*, 1909, oil on canvas, The Cleveland Museum of Art, Hinman B. Hurlbut Collection 1133.1922; © The Cleveland Museum of Art.

page 5: George Bellows, *Approach to the Bridge at Night*, 1913, oil on canvas, Chazen Museum of Art, University of Wisconsin–Madison, Gift of Mr. and Mrs. Gordon R. Walker, 1972.8.

pages 6–7: The Central (Columbus, Ohio) High School infield, c. 1900, George Bellows Papers, Amherst College Archives and Special Collections, Amherst, Massachusetts; by permission of the Trustees of Amherst College.

pages 8–9: George Bellows, *New York*, 1911, oil on canvas, National Gallery of Art, Washington, Collection of Mr. and Mrs. Paul Mellon, 1986.72.1.

page 10: Gertrude Käsebier, *Robert Henri*, c. 1907–08, platinum print, Delaware Art Museum, Gift of Helen Farr Sloan, 1978.

page 11: Robert Henri, *Snow in New York*, 1902, oil on canvas, National Gallery of Art, Washington, Chester Dale Collection, 1954.4.3.

page 12: George Bellows, *Cliff Dwellers*, 1913, oil on canvas, Los Angeles County Museum of Art, Los Angeles County Fund (16.4); © 2009 Museum Associates / LACMA / Art Resource, NY.

page 15: George Bellows, *Splinter Beach* in *The Masses* 4 (July 1913), pp. 10–11, Special Collections Research Center, The University of Chicago Library.

page 16: George Bellows, *Frankie, the Organ Boy*, 1907, oil on canvas, The Nelson-Atkins Museum of Art, Kansas City, Missouri. Purchase: acquired through the bequest of Ben and Clara Shlyen, F91-22; photograph Jamison Miller.

page 17: John Sloan, *Six O'Clock, Winter*, 1912, oil on canvas, The Phillips Collection, Washington, DC.

page 19: George Bellows, *North River*, 1908, oil on canvas, Pennsylvania Academy of the Fine Arts, Philadelphia, Joseph E. Temple Fund, 1909.2.

Bellows in his studio, 1908, George Bellows Papers, Amherst College Archives and Special Collections, Amherst, Massachusetts; by permission of the Trustees of Amherst College.

pages 20–21: George Bellows, *Emma at the Piano*, 1914, oil on panel, Chrysler Museum of Art, Norfolk, Virginia, Gift of Walter P. Chrysler, Jr., 71.617; © Courtesy of the Bellows Trust.

pages 22–23: George Bellows, *Blue Morning*, 1909, oil on canvas, National Gallery of Art, Washington, Chester Dale Collection, 1963.10.82.

pages 24–25: George Bellows, *The Lone Tenement*, 1909, oil on canvas, National Gallery of Art, Washington, Chester Dale Collection, 1963.10.83.

pages 26–27: George Bellows, *Both Members of This Club*, 1909, oil on canvas, National Gallery of Art, Washington, Chester Dale Collection, 1944.13.1.

page 29: George Bellows, *Real Tragedy* in *The Masses* 33 (February 1914), Special Collections Research Center, The University of Chicago Library.

page 30: George Bellows, *Lady Jean*, 1924, oil on canvas, Yale University Art Gallery, New Haven, bequest of Stephen Carlton Clark, B.A. 1903, 1961.18.7; Yale University Art Gallery / Art Resource, NY.

page 33: George Bellows, *Self-Portrait*, 1921, lithograph, Library of Congress Prints and Photographs Division, Washington, LC-USZ72-107; courtesy of the Library of Congress.

INDEX

Note: Page numbers in *italics* refer to illustrations.

For J. B. Daniel, artist with a touch

Library of Congress Cataloging-in-Publication Data

Burleigh, Robert.
George Bellows : painter with a punch! / by Robert Burleigh.
p. cm.
ISBN 978-1-4197-0166-5
1. Bellows, George, 1882–1925—Juvenile literature. 2. Painters—United
States—Biography—Juvenile literature. I. Bellows, George, 1882–1925.
II. Title. III. Title: Painter with a punch!
ND237.B45B87 2012
759.13--dc23
2011034276

Text copyright © 2012 Robert Burleigh
Illustration credits on page 37
Book design by Maria T. Middleton

Printed and bound in China
10 9 8 7 6 5 4 3 2 1

ABRAMS
THE ART OF BOOKS SINCE 1949
115 West 18th Street
New York, NY 10011
www.abramsbooks.com